Pinterest Affiliate Marketing

Best Social Media Platform to Make Passive Income Online

Thomas F. Hartley

Copyright © dsk-enterprise Inc Ltd., 2020

All rights reserved. No part of this publication may be reproduced in any form without written consent of the author and the publisher. The information contained in this book may not be stored in a retrieval system, or transmitted in any form by any means, electronic, mechanical, photocopying or otherwise without the written consent of the publisher. This book may not be resold, hired out or otherwise disposed by way of trade in any form of binding or cover other than that in which it is published, without the written consent of the publisher. Respective authors own all copyrights not held by the publisher. The presentation of the information is without contract or any type of guarantee assurance. All trademarks and brands within this book are for clarifying purposes only and are the owned by the owners themselves, not affiliated with this document.

Disclaimer

This document is geared towards providing exact and reliable information in regards to the topic and issue covered. The publication is sold with the idea that the publisher is not required to render accounting, officially permitted, or otherwise, qualified services. If advice is necessary, legal or professional, a practiced individual in the profession should be ordered. In no way is it legal to reproduce, duplicate, or transmit any part of this document in either electronic means or in printed format. Recording of this publication is strictly prohibited and any storage of this document is not allowed unless with written permission from the publisher. All rights reserved. The information provided herein is stated to be truthful and consistent, in that any liability, in terms of inattention or otherwise, by any usage or abuse of any policies, processes, or directions contained within is the solitary and utter responsibility of the recipient reader. Under no circumstances will any legal responsibility or blame be held against the publisher for any reparation, damages, or monetary loss due to the information herein, either directly or indirectly. The information herein is offered for informational purposes solely, and is universal as so. The presentation of the information is without contract or any type of guarantee assurance.

This book is not intended for use as a source of legal, medical, business, accounting or financial advice. All readers are advised to seek services of competent professionals in the legal, medical, business, accounting, and finance fields.

Introduction

Pinterest, a virtual and visual bulletin board website is now the talk of the town. If you must know, such social networking site has a million of users active. As it is all about images and videos, Pinterest users tend to express themselves through pinning images. Interaction is also present since users are allowed to comments of pins of the people the user follows.

The best thing about Pinterest is that it is also a free social networking site. What's more, marketers even use this platform to market their product or services using the right method. It is the place where people pin and repin images that interest them. Since it's Pinterest's goal is to connect people, marketers believe that it is the right place for them to get targeted traffic.

Table of Contents

1. Social Meida Guide: What Is Pinterest?

2. Are You Pinterested?

3. What Is Pinterest For Business?

4. How to Get More Followers on Pinterest

5. Pro's and Con's of Pinterest Marketing

6. How to Integrate Pinterest With Facebook Page

7. How to Use Pinterest for Your Blog, Business or Nonprofit

8. Augment Sales Revenues With Pinterest

Chapter I

Social Meida Guide: What Is Pinterest?

In today's world, social media has taken over! With a variety of different websites like Facebook, Twitter, LinkedIn, YouTube, even Google+, there are few people in the world who aren't somehow involved with the new trend. It seems as though everyone is always looking for the newest and hottest social media phenomenon. And if you've hit this article, you've found the new phenomenon! It is called Pinterest. But what is Pinterest and who is it for? Let's take a look at the who, what, when, why, and how of Pinterest to help you become more familiar with the latest social media trend.

What is Pinterest?

Pinterest, the latest social phenomena to hit the masses, is a sharing platform in which you "pin" pictures to your board. The picture sharing site allows you to create categories of photographs, pin your pictures, and share them with other people. In addition to pinning pictures, you can also pin videos, share monetary gifts, and join discussion groups.

When would you use pinterest?

Initially, Pinterest began as a type of scrapbooking website in which users could post pictures of their family, pets, or vacation and share them with others. As such, it was seen as more of a spare time or hobby type website. However, as the platform began to grow, users started to see the potential that it really held. With new features included, individuals are now using Pinterest for a wide variety of things such as wedding planning, interior decorating, and even marketing.

Who uses Pinterest?

Now that we have answered the questions "What is Pinterest?" and "When would you use Pinterest?", let's answer the question "Who uses Pinterest?" The answer to this question is simple - everyone and anyone. As stated previously, Pinterest started as a platform for everyday users who wanted to organize and share their pictures with the world. Since then, business owners have began to see the potential of the platform and are now using it to market their products and distribute their brand messages.

Why use Pinterest?

There are several different reasons that one might use Pinterest:

- To share photos with family and friends
- To share information - Many people use Pinterest to post their recipes and ideas, or showcase their talents through photographs.

- To gather inspiration - Individuals from around the world use Pinterest to showcase their best ideas. So whether you are looking for wedding ideas, cake ideas, decorating ideas, or other forms of inspiration, Pinterest is a great place to find it.
- To promote a business - Pinterest can be a great way to share your products with the world. Post your product pictures, or use Pinterest to showcase the talents that you have to offer. Even better, use it to create a visual brand personality for your business. Make people fall in love with who you are and what you do.

Now that you know "What is Pinterest?", who uses it, and why you would use it, there's one final question to answer:

How do you use Pinterest?

It's simple! Just head to the Pinterest website to learn how to set up an account.

Then follow people on Pinterest and enjoy the ride.

So what is Pinterest? It is the latest social media trend, allowing account owners to share and browse through pinboards of pictures.

Basic Pinterest Marketing Concepts

Pinterest is a great tool for marketing. Curiously, Pinterest marketing utilizes its native power to encourage people utilizing photos. It is the goal of Pinterest to connect people through things that have typical interests.

When engaging in your Pinterest marketing campaign it is crucial to avoid the magpie syndrome. Not just since Pinterest is brand-new you have to join in to be in the crowd. When you are marketing with Pinterest it is good to discover how the video game is played.

Contests. Contests are an excellent method of producing awareness and exposure for your item both in the online and offline world. The mechanics of joining your Pinterest contests need to be simple and every entry must be a sure winner. This will make people flock to your boards and follow you. The amount of eyeballs that will be considered for the contest is an incredible increase in offering your items and business more exposure.

This trick worked for Facebook and it will work for Pinterest too. Permit other Pinterest users to pin things on boards that you host. Individuals tend to emulate other individuals if you try to show off how beneficial your items can be for their lifestyle through images.

Produce original content. Let's face it. About 80 percent of the activities in Pinterest are driven by re-pins. This indicates that initial material has the possible to rule the Pinterest marketing universe. Original material has far more chances to be re-pinned than non-original content. This will provide a boost for your items direct exposure and awareness.

Be follow-worthy. Make your board worthy of following through believed provoking material. The more interesting your material becomes the much better opportunities that you will make more followers. Another thing to keep in mind so you 'd be follow-worthy is to first follow others. This is the principle that has actually been proven all across the social media galaxy., if you follow the leading pet dogs possibilities are they will follow you back.., if the top canine follows you the follow the leader syndrome kicks in which can earn you more eyeballs that will increase the presence of your items.

Your Pinterest marketing can become an excellent financial investment to make. The ?uantity of time and effort that you spend on Pinterest can make or break your marketing and the quantity of money that you will earn. The surest method to prosper in marketing in Pinterest is to invest a lot on research study and to learn the very best practices from other online marketers and even your rivals.

Pinterest is a good tool for marketing. When engaging in marketing in Pinterest it is essential to prevent the magpie syndrome. Your Pinterest marketing can end up being a great investment to make. The quantity of time and effort that you invest on Pinterest can make or break your marketing and the amount of cash that you will earn. The surest way to succeed in marketing in Pinterest is to invest a lot on research and to find out the finest practices from other marketers and even your competitors.

Chapter II

Are You Pinterested?

If you are going to embrace social media for promoting your business, consider including Pinterest as part of your marketing strategy.

Assess the Pinterest Option

Here are questions to ask yourself to help determine whether marketing with Pinterest might be of value to your business:

- Is your business B2B or B2C?
- Will you use Pinterest to get more traffic?
- Is your target customer mostly men or women?
- How do you think you will benefit from using Pinterest?
- Is your business, product or service-based?

- Are your products or services mostly related to fashion, weddings, cooking or crafts? »
- Do your products have strong visual appeal? (Do you have the time to improve the content and visual quality of your web and other social media sites, especially any photos?)
- Are you already using social media for business?
- Why are you interested in using Pinterest
- Will you pin items that aren't totally about your business (news, trends, others' ideas, etc.)?

If you have clear answers to all of these questions, you might find value in developing a Pinterest-based social media presence. However, if you are overwhelmed, annoyed, or burnt out on "yet another social media site", you might set Pinterest aside for a while.

What do you know about Pinterest?

Pinterest serves a slightly different function in social media. It is not the place where you converse to the same degree as with Facebook or Twitter and it is not another blog site. Pinterest is a social/visual "virtual pinboard" that allows users to post (pin) images or videos from the web to their own (and others' boards) and browse Pinterest.

Once a Pinterest account is created, virtual boards created within the account can be categorized and the user can add descriptions as reminders of why a picture or video was saved. Many (but not all) images/pins link the Pinterest user back to the website source for easy access at a later time. The account owner-user can invite others to pin content of related interest to the board, or can restrict it to personal use, only.

One media writer describes Pinterest as a "database « of intentions". An individual often uses his or her Pinterest board to collect ideas, specifically visual images, of something desired. For instance, you may want to see pictures of wedding gowns (a popular subject on Pinterest). Pictures of interest can be "pinned" to the board.

Many website images now include a Pin It widget on their pages enabling the visitor to pin content from that web page. And users can upload pins of their own content - the amazing dessert, an image of a newly-completed oil painting, or images of a new line of winter fashion accessories.

How Does Marketing Come Into This?

As a business promoter, your goal is to increase viewer traffic to your social media site. Once there, it is up to your web content to influence visitors to make purchases. Pinterest is now seen as an extension of an individual's or a company's website and it is credited with increasing page views by as much as 29 percent.

The increasingly popular Etsy online marketplace is considered to be one of the best performing brands on Pinterest, increasing Etsy's revenue by 9.4 percent in 2013. Why the interest? It's the pictures!

People love pictures in advertising for Do-It-Yourself (DIY) projects, and posted with crafts, how-to's and recipes. Viewers want pictures in all platforms. Brands need to incorporate pictures into Pinterest and all social media sites used for marketing.

Where to Start

- Knowledge - Start by building your knowledge base about the types of interests and prospective clients might use Pinterest.
- Pinterest has more than 70 million «sers. That's a large potential customer/consumer base.
- Women users repin (pinning images found on the web and in Pinterest

searches) to their own boards more often than men but have fewer followers.
- The top three most popular Pinterest categories are DIY and crafts, hair and beauty, and design.
- The most popular categories on Pinterest are babies, beauty, crafts, fashion, fitness, food, home décor, kids, pets, and travel. Seasonal subjects are very popular, too - holidays, seasonal changes, current events.
- Category usage differs vastly from men to women: women focus on fewer categories whereas men spread out their pins. Also, women's top five categories account for more than 56 percent of all their Pinterest activity; men's top five categories are under 40 percent.
- Men users favor photography, art, design, and home décor categories.

- Time of day for pinning can be important. In the United States, the best time of day to pin is between 2 PM and 4 PM (Eastern time); the best time at night is between 8 PM and 1 AM (Eastern time).

Do extensive online research. Look at some of the popular retail sites and notice their use of PinIt widgets. Search the Internet for subjects from one of the more popular categories. Your search will probably bring up Pinterest links. Click and view the subject on the Pinterest site and study the content, layout, and appearance.

Create a Pinterest account and get verified through the site's business section. You can set up your Pinterest boards privately, adjusting them until you believe you have them ready for show. Then, « change the viewing status and start monitoring your PinIt results.

You will have access to some interesting business development tools, including analytics. Use the analytics tool to see pin activity data on your website and Pinterest boards. The analytics can help you better understand what pinners like ("Most Repinned and Most Clicked). Customize and fine-tune your pins for more conversions.

Your clients are exploring your site for items to pin and repin to other Pinterest boards. You should be focused on creating content that reflects your customer's passions. Pinterest users typically share content that has educational value and practicality to them. How can you align your content to the customers' interests?

Preparing Your Pinterest Content

- Website evaluation - Is your website Pin-friendly, up-to-date, and current content rich, especially with quality pictures? Get your website in good order.

- Content organization - Organize all your Pinterest boards by themes to make it easier for other users to find and browse specific content.
- Brand the photos - Brand (add your logo) to a corner of each picture you pin to your board. Researchers have noted that large watermarks over images are Pinner turnoffs.
- Shopper-friendly content - More than most social media sites, Pinterest is about shopping. Each board should

Shopper-friendly content - More than most social media sites, Pinterest is about shopping. Each board should be designed and content-filled with "shopper friendly" in mind. Describe the product or service and use only clear, quality images.

- Join the community - while you spend time each day updating and checking your social media, engage with the people of the communities:

post and answer questions, and comment on others' content.
- Repin - When it comes directly to Pinterest, invite others to repin content to your board. Repinning to your account brings your account to the attention of the person from whom you repined (that person receives a notification and/or email). The person from whom you repined may also return the repin favor.
- No broken backlinks - make sure your links in Pinterest correctly backlink to your web, Facebook or Twitter sites. Fix any broken backlinks!

Picture Clear

Let's get clear on pictures. There are some key points to know about posting pictures and videos on Pinterest:

- Brand images (on Pinterest) are more likely to receive a repin if the

image does not contain a face - 23 percent more likely. BTW, one study showed that Pinterest has 4.25 times more images without faces.
- Color - images with lots of color are preferred. Red, orange and brown images are twice as likely to be repined; blue images are less likely. Images with medium lightness will be repinned 20 times more often than mostly black images, eight times more likely than white images.
- Background and texture - influence repinning choices. Pinsters favour images with less than 30 percent background; the drop-« off rate was two-to-four times for images that contain 40 percent or more background content. Smooth textures are preferred to rough textures - garnering up to 17 times more repins.
- Image size - taller images and vertical images are more repinable

according to studies. Smaller images and infographics receive more click-throughs because they are harder to read from the Pinterest site. An infographic headline is key to getting more click throughs.
- Traffic response - you can control traffic response by including a specific call to action on your pin's landing page

Maintaining Your Presence

A large business with its own marketing group or consultants can spend a considerable amount of time studying the analytics on ROI, placing the most professionally done photographs and text and updating content nearly every day.

The smaller business person should plan to spend at least two hours daily, monitoring feedback, replying to comments (when appropriate), and refreshing content. This is a fairly small investment of time and effort for potentially good results.

Over time, the comments and number of visitors will begin to show what areas of your content are effective - like what products are being ignored and which are being purchased. Conversely, they may reveal lack of interest and a limited number of purchases.

If your traffic remains sluggish, evaluate every aspect - text, layout, images, links - everything. You may want or need to consult with an online marketing specialist or web/media designer for assistance in refreshing your content.

It's easy to overwhelm viewers with information and oversaturation is as ineffective in marketing as is too little valuable content. Again, feedback will let you know what's working and what isn't.

One more thing about those numbers - marketers can buy "likes" and "tweets" to inflate the numbers of legitimate viewer likes and tweets. Those high numbers you envy may not necessarily be an accurate representation of who is really following a brand. More importantly, they don't accurately represent the purchases related to that brand.

Chapter III

What Is Pinterest For Business?

Pinterest for Business is an easy way for businesses to inspire their community and direct consumers to your website or blog. You can highlight important aspects of your brand that consumers may not have considered. Pinterest is a tool that will allow you to easily see what your consumers want and like.

There are many useful tools to promote your product, company or service. Using the Pinterest Pin Count tool will allow you to view the number of times a page or blog post from your site has been pinned or repinned within Pinterest.

Be Interactive

You need to be interactive in your posts to gain popularity on Pinterest. Pinterest is a great platform for you to reach your target users. One way of doing so is by replying to comments on your posts and submitting comments on others posts that are related to your business or product. The more interactive you are, the more likely it is for you to gain popularity.

Selling your Product

Here are a few simple tips for promoting your company, product or service on Pinterest.

Use images that portray your company, product or service in a positive light. When adding items to Pinterest, use good quality images.

Placing the product correctly counts for a lot. Create boards and pins that are not about selling but display your product, company or service in the photo.

Make is easy for pinners to buy your product or service. When you pin an enticing item, consumers need to know where to buy it. Consumers should be lead to a sales page where details on purchasing are provided.

Use enticing words and phrases. If you are pinning food use words that will make the potential purchases hungry (succulent, mouth-watering, etc).

Don't spam. If you spam or push sales to your consumers, you will not gain any consumers or you may earn a bad reputation.

Reach Out Creatively

As said earlier, you can reach out to your users numerous ways using Pinterest. Use your creativity to reach out to your users through pins. You could start a lucky draw contest for people who share a certain picture of your specific product. Use creative images, videos and other items to make your profile unique and attractive. According to the statistics, 69% of Pinterest users bought at least one item on the website. As a business owner, you surely don't want to miss on such an opportunity.

Speak In Users' Common Language

Now, this doesn't mean you should write captions on your pictures in different languages for your users to read. It simply means that you should see what's "trending" nowadays and market your product accordingly. You could make creative memes about your product or use your slogan for info-graphics.

Make Different Pin Boards for Different Products

Along with a parent page for your company, make separate boards for each product. This will help you reach out better to your targeted users, benefitting your brand. Profile images look best at 160 x 165 pixels.

A few simple rules to remember to make your Board stand out from others.

Remember to put your pinners first. Tailor your pinning to the pinners you are want to attract.

Create a Board to allow others to see what inspires your work. Don't be afraid to share a painting or design that inspired your work.

Be authentic, just like your pinners. Be creative, be yourself and have fun pinning!

21 Pinterest Marketing Tricks

Pinterest is one of the most powerful mediums you can use to attract massive traffic to your website. In addition, it allows you to tap into 176,000,000 users for free. In fact, studies have shown that 18% of the Pinterest users have the average income of $75,000 and higher. It means that there are potential clients you can tap into for your business.

Furthermore, with the power of Pinterest, you can utilize images, private messages, as well as videos to direct people to your website, YouTube videos, or any posts of your choice. This allows you to bring massive traffic to your landing page in which you are able to build massive subscribers base for your business on a daily basis.

Remember, your formula will always be... Visitors ---> Build Subscribers --> Potential Customers ---> Relationship Building ---> Revenue For Your Business. That's exactly the power of Pinterest Marketing.

Here come some suggestions and tricks to put you on the right track:

Trick #1: Blast Emails to your list. -- Instead of just following others on Pinterest, send emails to your list and let them know that you are going to share cool tips and tricks on solving their problems on your Pinterest page.

Trick #2: Follow 300 Pinterest Users in Your Niche every day. -- Even though this technique is a little outdated, but in reality, it will seduce other users to follow you on Pinterest.

Trick #3: Pin 30 to 40 Pictures Per Day. -- However, you need to focus on those users in your niche. Even though this is a broad strategy, in reality, it will help you get followers to your Pinterest account.

Trick #4: Remove Pinterest users who don't follow you back. -- You need to wait roughly about one week before you remove any users you follow on Pinterest. Why is this important? Well, you want to work with only users who will reciprocate with you.

Trick #5: Put a Pinterest Button on your website. -- This allows other Pinterest users to share your blog or squeeze page for free.

Trick #6: Add Pinterest Pictures As a Journey of Your Venture. -- You can add a daily picture to your Pinterest as a way to tell your audience what you do on a daily basis. This allows your audience to see your daily activities in the form of pictures.

Trick #7: Greet each new followers that follow you on Pinterest. -- This allows you to have a lasting impression with each audience that could be potential customers for your business.

Trick #8: Make Friends with some Pinterest users. -- Why is this important? Well, when you make friends with 10 top Pinterest marketers, you are able to work together on pin each other posts. This allows you to build viral traffic within each other business.

This allows you to tag their name every time you post on Instagram.

Trick #9: Take pictures on certain friends who have Pinterest account. -- The idea is the same as Trick #8. The concept is to make sure that you looked famous in front of your audience. HINT: You can always attend a seminar and take pictures with the attendees.

Trick #10: Add signature file for every outgoing email. -- You just need to mention something like... "P.S. You can always follow my every move on Pinterest at {{Your PINTEREST URL}}".

Trick #11: Create A Special Discount in Exchange to Following You on Pinterest. -- Create a *SPARK* and incentive for your audience to Follow you on Pinterest.

Example:

Create a contest where you can ask your audience to click on the "Follow" button to get a coupon code for a 90% discount on your latest product at $99. (Well, it doesn't matter whether it is $99 product or $10 product. My point is... "Utilize the special discount".

Trick #12: Comment on each Pinterest posts in your niche. -- You should only comment on the posts in your niche. For Example: If you are in the weight loss niche, only comment on the post within that particular niche. When you stay focus on that particular niche, you are able to maximize the results.

Trick #13: Create A Cash Contest. -- You can use *real* cash as part of your contest where you ask people to follow you or engage conversation with your post on Pinterest. In addition, you can also provide *gift certificate* that can be used to purchase your product.

Example:

1st Winner = $100 + $500 Gift Certificates to YOURPRODUCTS.

2nd Winner = $75 + $400 Gift Certificates to YOURPRODUCTS.

3rd Winner = $50 + $250 Gift Certificates to YOURPRODUCTS.

4th Winner = $25 + $150 Gift Certificates to YOURPRODUCTS.

5th Winner = $75 Gift Certificates to YOURPRODUCTS.

Trick #14: Brand Your Name First. -- It is important to brand your name such as: JaredAnderson. This allows you to build your reputation as a public figure where you will attract loyal followers for your business.

Trick #15: Brand Your Business After You Brand Your Name. -- Let people get to know first. Once they do, people will want to get to know your company and the progress within your company.

Remember: Pinterest vision is all about photos and videos sharing. It means that when you brand YOU with photos and videos, you will create a higher engagement. This allows people want to connect with your business. It is that powerful

Trick #16: Schedule Your Weekly Posts Ahead of Time. -- Instead of scheduling your weekly posts on a daily basis. You need to come up with all posts for a specific week one week at a time. This way, you will be able to stay productive on other tasks for your business.

Trick #17: Target Buyer Keywords At All Costs. -- Which one is more profitable? Wedding consultants or Wedding articles?

When someone chooses "wedding consultant", do you consider this person as someone who is ready to purchase?

When someone chooses "wedding articles", do you consider this person as someone who is ready to purchase?

Of course, the answer is obvious. When people choose "wedding consultant", they are looking for a consultant. It means that they are READY to pay $$$. My point is for you to look deeper into your niche. This allows you to focus on a pot of gold rather than just a pot of pebble.

Trick #18: Track Your Link At All Cost. -- If you don't track, you lose cash. I know it is easy to feel that you don't have the time. However, if you don't track your link, you won't be able to know which produces more clicks and which wall post give you a lower conversion.

Trick #19: Always Use Your Squeeze Page URL on Your Profile Description. -- This allows you to build your subscriber base from Pinterest. Always remember that your goal from Pinterest marketing is to build your list first. NOTE: Studies have shown that each subscriber that you have is equal to $1 to $1.50 per month for your business.

Trick #20: Always Use Images that focus on the result you want your audience have. -- Images are more powerful than words. Use them to show your audience what they can get if they utilize your products and services.

Trick #21: If you have nothing new to post, you can always publish image with a motivational quote. -- With so many negativities around us, motivational quotes will attract your audience to follow you on Pinterest. (Yes, you can always gram motivational quotes as often as you wish!)

Chapter IV

How to Get More Followers on Pinterest

Pinterest - the internet's latest public press trend, is a fantastic way to develop attention for your web or blogsite. But as with most public press marketing methods, your ability to impact others through your Pinterest existence is limited if you do not have that many individuals following you in the first position.

So today, I'll discuss a few methods that can be effective for developing up your Pinterest following. Try applying a few of these thoughts to your own Pinterest user profile and watch your variety of supporters soar!

Tip #1 - Tie In to Your Current Social Networks

One of the quickest and simplest methods to get more Pinterest supporters is by attaching your consideration to your current Facebook or MySpace and Tweets information. Doing so (and setting up your authorizations correctly) means that every new item you pin will be shown to your supporters on these systems. Since you already have established relationships with members on these websites, you will discover that many of them tend to adhere to along with your Pinterest user profile naturally.

Tip #2 - Create it Easy to Pin Your Content

Integrating Pinterest control buttons into your content, product pages and other areas of your web page can help boost frequent your articles is pinned and lead to new supporters for your user profile. Because Pinterest is still relatively new, basically having these control buttons in position provides a visible memory for individuals to sign up to your user profile and interact with your articles on this new web page.

Tip #3 - Create Forums to Supplement Your Posts

Alternatively, why not develop a Pinterest panel that is built around one of your content. For example, if you run a dog training tips web page and suggest several different items in a new writing, develop a Pinterest panel linked with this post that stocks these suggestions in a visible way. Doing so creates your articles more interesting and gives visitors a purpose to adhere to along with your user profile.

Tip #4 - Pin Regularly

As with any public press web page, identifying how often to pin new articles includes finding the ideal balance between publishing so little that there is no value in following your user profile and publishing so often that individuals get frustrated with your continuous updates. For best results, aim to pin between 5-30 new items a day, with regards to the variety of active Pinterest boards you maintain.

Tip #5 - Improve Your Board Labeling Structure

Giving each panel on your Pinterest user profile a fun and exclusive, but easy to understand, name is an important part of gaining new supporters. Since many members tend to only adhere to it's that are most appropriate to them, it's essential that your panel brands allow it to be instantly obvious what each of your boards are about.

Consider the following example given by Angie, a Pinterest user running a blog on the web page Many Little Blessings:

"A panel about day workouts could be named "Morning Routines" or "Morning

To Dos," but if you name it "Rise and Glow," individuals will know it has something to do with days, but no concept that it's day routine thoughts."

Tip #6 - Curate Your Own Pins

If you only ever repin articles from others, you are not bringing anything new to the table, which gives Pinterest customers even less of a motivation to adhere to along with you. Instead, build your own new hooks based on articles you discover on other internet websites or from resources you are familiar with that have not yet been presented substantially on Pinterest.

Tip #7 - Follow Other Pinners

On Pinterest - as on Tweets, Google+ and Facebook or MySpace - following other customers (especially power customers with countless numbers and a large number of exclusive subscribers) is a fantastic way to get your articles observed and propagate across a much bigger network of individuals. To discover other pinners to adhere to along with, look for a few of your industry's general keywords and words on Pinterest and take note of the customers that appear to post the most articles and have the most supporters. Follow these customers yourself and repin some of their articles - many will return the benefit by following you back and giving your hooks with their networks!

Tip #8 - Arrange a Pin Exchange

While it's considered incorrect to pin your own articles too frequently, you can always team up with other internet marketers or suppliers in your market to arrange a "pin exchange" that allows more of your articles to be seeded on to Pinterest without your direct participation. A band of friends who all sell items on Etsy, for example, could arrange to discuss each other person's articles on Pinterest to be able to develop acknowledgement without showing too "scammy".

Tip #9 - Increase Your Boards

It should go without saying, but when you offer plenty of different boards across a wide range of passions and subjects, you are developing more opportunities for individuals to adhere to along with you. While it's a wise decision to develop boards that are appropriate to your web page or business, consider developing boards on your personal passions and activities as well to reach a bigger individuals.

Tip #10 - Pin Newsworthy Content

As mentioned in Tip #6, if you want to develop your variety of Pinterest supporters, it's essential that you be seen as a "thought leader" in your market - not just someone who repins articles from other individuals. To increase this understanding, try to be the first to develop hooks for news items within your market. You could even create boards to function new items that are launched in your niche, making you the "go to" pinner providing your field.

Tip #11 - Use Pinterest to Create Tutorials

People love tech tutorials, and the exclusive visible display of Pinterest creates it preferably suited to develop lessons that other customers can adhere to. As an example, say you run a web page that instructs online marketing to internet marketers. Using Pinterest, you could develop a "step-by-step" guide panel, in which you function links to different articles from around the web on subjects like choosing online items and programs to market, developing traffic to your web page and enhancing alterations. Create lessons on subjects that you know will interest folks and you are sure to pick up more supporters for your consideration.

Tip #12 - Write Retrievable Pin Captions

One of the methods that individuals new Pinterest customers to adhere to along with is by searching the web page for interesting key words to be able to find new pinned articles. If your hooks do not appear in these looks, you are losing potential supporters that could have decided upon your boards. Because of this, it's essential to include appropriate keywords and words into your pin sayings. Don't basically stuff your hooks full of useless keywords and words, but at the same time, do not use basic sayings like, "So funny!" that do not give Pinterest customers or the website look for engine optimization any information about what exactly is going on in your hooks.

Tip #13 - Use Excellent Pictures

Pinterest is visually-focused web page, the caliber of the images you use in your hooks will go a long way towards gaining new supporters. If the Pinterest bookmarklet does not instantly catch an eye-catching picture (or, if there are useless images used on the source articles page in the first place), personally result in the pin on your own using a excellent, creatively eye-catching picture from a Creative Commons picture index.

Chapter V

Pro's and Con's of Pinterest Marketing

In today's Internet world, social marketing sites have become more and more popular. These social networking sites allow people to connect through words, pictures, sounds and even videos. People can connect anytime and anywhere. Pinterest is a major player in social media with over 13 million users and they have caught the attention of marketers. It is a social-sharing photo website allowing you to "Pin" images to virtual pin boards in order to get your pins noticed and share them with your followers. Users organize, share and store pictures uploaded. Currently, Pinterest is popular among consumer marketers, but should B2B marketers use the platform in their social media strategies? Let's consider the Pro's and Con's of Pinterest marketing.

Pro's of Pinterest Marketing

- Easy to Use - The Pinterest site is easy to both use and to navigate. The best Pinterest marketing strategy for newcomers to the site is the making of files accessible with just a click on a pin and allowing users to share the pins they like on the marketer's business profile.
- Generates Referral Traffic - More referral traffic is generated by Pinterest than many major social networking sites.
- Content is Visual - Since Pinterest is based on photo-sharing, the best Pinterest marketing strategy for sellers is to upload an outstanding picture of their product or service. They should also add their store's information to the picture's caption and promote the pin to other boards.

Pinterest pinning tips include the suggestion of being organized with your brand by your creating a design that will categorize your products into the boards. This will eliminate difficulty of clients to browse what you are offering.

- Market Research - Pinterest will not only give you opportunities for market exposure, but it will also provide a platform for market research to improve your advertising strategies. It allows you to interact with regular Pinterest members. By seeing their pins and comments, you will learn the kinds of things they are interested in. This knowledge will help you to develop a marketing campaign that will target the correct demographics.
- Ideal for Artistic Exposure - If you are a business such as architecture, interior design, fashion design or other similar industries, you will

find Pinterest the ideal site to exhibit your work online. The best way for you to get your pins noticed is to keep your content and posts eye-catching, original and high in quality.

- SEO - A Pinterest pinning tip includes an awareness that Pinterest builds a stored link for every user post. The stored links are inbound links to your site. Furthermore, the inbound links will raise your search engine ranking.
- Women Users - It has been said that 65% of Pinterest users are women and 85% of Pinterest traffic is driven by women. Therefore, if your business clients are women, Pinterest could be an excellent way to reach your potential customers.

Con's of Pinterest Marketing

- Copyright Issues - There can be copyright issues caused by many

users pinning and re-pinning images owned by others. Some legal bloggers have conveyed concerns for these possible copyright issues.
- Large Number of Women Users - If your interests are guy interests such as power tools or football, you probably won't find many images to your liking on Pinterest. If your demographic target isn't women, you may not be successful with Pinterest marketing.
- Not Business Oriented - Being repeatedly pinned may not help your business marketing even if the pin goes viral. The link to your site can be lost through the repeated re-pinning process and more traffic will not be drawn to your business site. Also, the focus on Pinterest is often on lifestyle content with items such as recipes, home décor and fashion.

Chapter VI

How to Integrate Pinterest With Facebook Page

If you have a Facebook business page and Pinterest business account - why not integrate both in a mutually beneficial strategy? If you have a following or one or both of the platforms, you can build up on that on other social media tools. There's no need to start from scratch, but it does need some careful planning to avoid just spamming your followers with similar messages on all social networks. And that's what I'm going to talk about in this post.

In June 2013, Pinterest had 70 million users, according to Paris-based social media research firm Semiocast. Businesses have a lot to gain from Pinterest (and social media in general): new customers, more engaged customers, sales. According to a June 2013 report by market intelligence firm Visioncritical, 4 in 10 social media users have purchased an item online or in store after "favoriting" or sharing it on Pinterest, Twitter, or Facebook. Nearly half - 47 percent - of Pinterest purchasers say they pinned and purchased something after simply stumbling across it on the site, not because of a focused search for the item.

So how can you get help from your Facebook fans to build a following on Pinterest? And how to integrate Pinterest with Facebook page? Here are some tips to get you started.

Get a Pinterest tab on you Facebook business page

1. Install an app on your Facebook page Pinterest tab, or use woobox.com. Woobox is the app that allows you to create your Pinterest page tab on your Facebook Page. You're allowed one free Pinterest tab, after that it's $29/month per Page for all the apps you want to use.

2. Create a tab for your Facebook page so when people come to read your posts, or find out about you they will also see that you are on Pinterest. The tab allows followers to view all your boards that are on Pinterest while remaining on the Facebook platform (woobox only), they are only taken to Pinterest when they repin or comment.

Additionally, with woobox you can require users to like your Facebook page before viewing your Pinterest tab, show all of your boards and pins styled just like they are on Pinterest, and get complete stats for page views, visits, and likes, segmented by fans and non-fans who view your tab.

Post Pinterest links as updates on Facebook Page

Share the direct link to your Pinterest page as a status update, let people know why they should follow you on both platforms. Be specific about the type of value you are creating on Pinterest for your followers.

Do it more than once - use different board visuals and different messages, to test what works. With only a fraction of your fans online at each moment in time, you can't expect all of them to notice this from just a single update and take action - follow you on Pinterest!

Promote specific boards on Facebook

On Pinterest followers can chose whether to follow all of your boards or just a few, and with this in mind - you may be more successful promoting specific boards to your Facebook followers. You might have board related to a specific product or service, business and non-business related boards, boards related to your other businesses or passions - not everything might be of interest or relevant to your fans. So test a few and see what works.

Update your status by uploading an image of a pin to Facebook, add description and add a link to the relevant board. A compelling image is given more space on Facebook newsfeed than just a link - so your update is more likely to get seen by your fans.

Post a link to your Pinterest board as a status update with an image of one of your pins. This will automatically generate an image. A full board preview can be generated by posting the board's direct URL, this will also include the text in your board description (you can set and change it in board's settings on Pinterest).

Don't forget to write a full description when setting up your boards and make use of the space beneath the board title. If you haven't done this when setting up your boards, it's easy to edit them now.

Promoting a particular pin

In the same way as promoting a particular board, a specific pin can be used, chose one which highlights the value you are providing.

Posting a direct link to a pin will automatically produce an image of the pin, the name of the board and the caption given. Optimise title and caption for impact - to grab attention, convey value and use the right keywords.

Promote Pinterest contests on Facebook

Contests and promotions are very popular on Pinterest, just as they are on Facebook. They are an effective way to drive traffic to your site and increase your followers. There are very few restrictions regarding the way contests and promotions are hosted on Pinterest, so get leverage from both platforms by promoting your Pinterest contest or promotion on Facebook and encourage your fans to take part. This could be that "carrot" they need to finally take action and follow your boards on Pinterest.

You can check out the latest brand guidelines for running a content on Pinterest here.

Another benefit of a Pinterest content - it creates a lot of engagement between your followers and this will usually translate to increased engagement on your Facebook page. Higher engagement on your Facebook page would result in Facebook treating your other updates more favourably in the newsfeed battle for space and reach. So a possible side effect - your Facebook engagement and reach will grow too.

What kind of content can you run on Pinterest?

Check these examples on pin-boards here and here. And this Hubspot's review of 8 Pinterest contests that worked (and why!).

And there is an app for that too... use woobox, shortstack or wishpond to manage your contest. Alternatively, you can create a minisite/landing page on your website to explain the details of your contest, how to enter, T&Cs and keep everyone updated on the progress.

Key elements of a successful Pinterest contest

Offer a reasonable prize that will motivate your followers to take action, the more you offer - the more action you could ask them to take to enter;

Your services could be used a prize too - design services, personal styling, SEO review etc.;

Ask entrants to follow you on Pinterest in order to build your following;

Ask them to create a board of a specific name and description, this will promote your contest to followers of the person who entered;

Ask them to pin at least ten items to that board to create a particular theme, several items must be from your website - this will share your content with a wide audience and create backlinks to your content;

Entrants must submit the board's URL on a form or by email (like the example above) and ask them to opt in to newsletter sign up - and build your email list at the same time.

If you put your contest information and entry form behind the "like-gate" on Facebook you could build your Facebook fanbase too - but beware of creating too many "hoops" for your entrants to jump through, or you won't get enough entries!

Ensure that your contest is mobile-friendly - most users of Facebook and Pinterest are on mobile phones, so they need to be able to access your "submission" tab or form in order to enter;

Ensure that your rules are clear in your Terms and Conditions, including the judging criteria, especially if you promote or run the contest as a Facebook app;

By spreading the word via social media, blog and your newsletter, you will also be encouraging your existing followers to engage with you on another social network.

Don't let it go on too long - 2 weeks is sufficient time for a contest to gain momentum and enough entries to make a decision;

Consider your target market - what would encourage them to spend time playing around with pins and creating a new board. If you are a fashion boutique, asking them to create a board that symbolizes the Autumn 2013 look best could work well and your judging criteria would reward interpretation of the latest fashions and creativity.

Your action this week:

if you have a Pinterest account, install a Pinterest tab on Facebook;

use status updates to promote boards and pins;

ensure descriptions, titles, and captions are optimised on your boards - and images from your website have links back to the site;

plan your Pinterest/Facebook marketing strategy - what updates you will post and how you will add value.

Chapter VII

How to Use Pinterest for Your Blog, Business or Nonprofit

Pinterest offers hope to the world of online marketing in many ways, offering a great way to increase the potency of your website traffic. The platform is very user-friendly and built to highlight the best content from your website. Any website that does commerce online can benefit from creating an active Pinterest presence, although not every website should use Pinterest in the exact same way.

Pinterest provides a place for you to collect and gather your own links, broken down by the categories you choose. In other words, it's all about deep-linking and hand-created indexing. The visual aspect is similar to an online scrapbook or collage, which is why users are so highly addicted to it! Pinterest is a universe of wish lists, favorite clothing, beautiful ideas and well-curated content. It's a marketer's dream.

One of the best features of Pinterest is its ability to build a highly -motivated audience through "repins" -- which are essentially users that reblog your content and move it onto a board that's all their own. Users are quite adept at finding new niches that you hadn't thought of appealing to, and retailers often find their products cater to certain groups that they may have overlooked.

If you're not sure how to use Pinterest to amplify your website's visibility, traffic or increase your sales, here's a quick primer, broken by website type.

Pinterest for Bloggers

While Pinterest typically focuses on images, many bloggers have found success by targeting their audience by starting boards on their favorite topics to write on. Pinterest does best with content that is easy to share. It's an excellent idea to look for other bloggers to connect with via Pinterest and ask them to share a board. By using board sharing, you will be able to have other contribute to your Pinterest board, creating fresh content for your active followers without having to blog all day.

Because Pinterest is a visual social media network, you'll only be able to post blog postings with visual images. The search engines dig visual content, too, so if you've been writing text blog posts without any images, now is the time to invest in some good stock art!

Headlines are often as important as the image you choose. Pinterest allows you to write your own headlines and doesn't pull that content from your blog. Be creative and experiment with different headlines. You can't go wrong by offering the answer to an intriguing question or promising "the world's best" brownie recipe. It's also the perfect venue to launch memes about your brand or product.

Pinterest for Businesses

Businesses can take one of two approaches to their pins. It's fairly easy to categorize your products and approach Pinterest as an enormous online catalog by pinning your products one by one. In fact, many companies join Pinterest as a business account and choose Pinterest to announce new products and sales.

Other businesses use a different approach. They create boards based on themes and sometimes invite their users to participate in pinning. Sometimes businesses set up boards with recipes from their activse followers or hold photo contests. The more you engage, the more likely that people will follow your business on Pinterest, and become interested, maybe even intrigued, by your brand.

If you want to fund real success using Pinterest, don't merely pin your products and forget about them. Find a better way. If you're selling services, don't pin an icon of the word "SEO" - nobody will want to repin that type of image, and you won't actively engage with others. If you're a tree removal company, highlight the biggest, baddest tree you've had to haul away. If you sell gourmet food, pin recipes and photos of foodie creations. If you sell business service, create fun memes and infograpics that highlight problems and solutions. If you're a retailer, create boards highlighting decorations for fantasy rooms. Set up boards for seasons and holidays. Invite users to upload pins of your products in use.

Pinterest allows retailers to list dollar amounts for the products you choose to showcase, but don't pin them all at once because they will get lost in an avalanche of other products. Choose a few produts to highlight each day, and pin them to every board you can. The best thing about this feature is that people will click, and buy.

Pinterest for Nonprofits

Nonprofits can make a great case for their cause using Pinterest. Make sure your content is pin-worthy, both interesting, eye catching, and unique. Pinterest should reflect your mission statement with appropriate boards that show the problems your organization seeks to solve.

Boards for nonprofits should be filled with hope, information, and action. highlight your nonprofit delivering vital services. Create infographics and memes that explain why your nonprofit is needed. Show off your events and your staff's smiling faces.

Don't forget that Pinterest allows users to showcase items for sale. Nonprofits can set up donations in this way by adding a dollar amount to uploaded images. Use the most compelling images you have and tell users where that $25 donation will go - to buy a pair of shoes, feed a hungry family in New York, or send a lifeline to a struggling soldier in Iraq.

As you can see, Pinterest is a versatile and fun social network where it's all about what you can show the world. Cultivate relationships with other users and join shared baords to maximize your exposure. Because of its addicting nature, you'll soon find that users from across the world are "loving" your pins and leaving comments that give you insight into future promotion efforts. Make sure that you monitor your growth, keep tabs on what works, and continue to pin all of your visually-appealing content on a regular basis to keep your followers engaged and drive traffic to your website.

Chapter VIII

Augment Sales Revenues With Pinterest

Pinterest has become a giant force in the social media world and it is gaining great influence not just in introducing innovative products for the customers in a visual business place, but also in growing sales. Various research prove the solid impact of Pinterest on the buying behavior of the customers. Wishpond reports that the Pinterest referrals astoundingly spend 70 percent more as compared to all other social media referrals. Another report from ComScore says that Pinterest customers expend more money, too often and on far great number of items, as compared to top social media websites. This is quite motivating for anyone who is aiming to become a valuable part of this wonderful social media community and get amazing benefits.

What is unique in Pinterest? Why does Pinterest attract a large number of buyers?

Actually, people are stimulated to buy due to visual appeal. We are very much interested to see the looks of a product, the way it works and the methods to use it. More importantly, we are happy to realize that our things are liked and are also attractive for other people as well. This knowledge of appreciation by others encourages us to know more about the latest growing trends and enable us to update ourselves about the next prominent thing that we can utilize.

Pinterest is designed in a perfect way to fulfill all those requirements and being an owner of a small business, you can acquire certain benefits with it. Pinterest can be used significantly to generate a large selection of wish lists for generating the desire for your products in the customers' mind. Check out the following to know how you can sign up and get maximum output from a Pinterest Business account.

How to Get Started? - Making a Pinterest Business Account

Convert your existing personal Pinterest account to a business account or set up a new business account. (The business accounts offer various tool and there are excellent benefits attached to this account that are outlined later in the article)

Choose a username. Username is unique for every user, offering a name length of 3-15 characters. (You must use keywords that relate to your business in the URL. This will enable you to improve your search engine rankings)

- Complete the profile information.
- Basic Information part
- Email notices

- Add links of other social media networks like Facebook, Twitter.

Upload profile picture for Pinterest Home page (Profile images are square on Pinterest). Pinterest chooses the centre square of images apart from of the content. Therefore, if you are using a portrait image as a head shot, only some part of your face will be visible in the profile, so before uploading the image, try to adjust the image size and make it into a square format. Keep in mind that this account is about your business. You may choose to pin images that are fun but your profile image must be very professional, so you can either choose the logo of the company or a very decent professional headshot.

Enter a Profile name

Enter complete details in the 'About Description' section. (For description, you have a limit of 200 characters but ensure that you include main keywords relating your business in order to maximize the optimization opportunities)

Install 'Pin it' button on to your bookmark toolbar.

Account Verification

Email- You must verify this requirement by using your email before you begin working on Pinterest.

Website- Pinterest enables the business users to include the address of their website in the public profile. The verified websites include a red check mark telling others that the website is complete safe to visit. This builds your confidence immediately.

Start Building Your Boards

Open 'Create a Board' link.

Enter a name of your board (For maximizing the Pinterest appeal, choose unique and interesting board names, attractive titles and have a balanced mix of social as well as business boards. Inspiration, Pets, Travel, Holiday (Christmas, Easter etc), Tutorials, DIYs are good options for social boards. Also, create boards to market and showcase your business products, services, professional help and customer tips etc.)

Complete the 'Board Description' (Remember to use keywords as the description is also searchable)

Choose a category for your board (Once you put the board in a particular category, it will be visible to other people who are not your followers when they browse through a category. Otherwise, limited people can view your pins in contrast to your board or profile followers.

Make your board either secret or public. The secret boards are visible only to people whom you invite and it cannot be searched. You have the option of making a secret board public, but you cannot use a public board as a secret one.

Create at least 5 boards having an excellent range of themes; ideally, each board must be having at minimum 15-20 images.

Add Images - 'Pinning'

Preferably, you must look to add 5-10 images every day. Doing this will not only keep the profile active and fresh, it will be beneficial for followers and fan base to keep visiting your boards; especially, if the content is informative and amusing. (Certain websites like PinGraphy.com offer paid services that allows the users to automatically schedule and pin pictures at the chosen date and time, meaning that you have to upload images in one bulk lot and the website will automatically take care of the next steps).

You have the option to add an image (called as a 'PIN') to your boards from a variety of sources:

Choose From Pinterest Search

- Find image for pinning
- Click on 'Pin It'
- Choose any of you boards from the 'Board' dropdown
- Enter description
- Click on the red 'Pin it' button
- Add From Your Pinterest Board

Click 'Add a Pin' button.

You can add images from your computer, from any website or from the Pinterest website (When you pin you own image, ensure that there is a proper file name as on Pinterest the name of the file becomes the image title.

Choose a board to pin image from dropdown. When you pin an image to any of your business boards, remember to take complete benefit of keywords to be added in the description box as well as the title.

Add From Online Sources

- Search an image you wish to add as a pin
- Click on the Pin it button on your bookmark toolbar
- Select the image
- Select the board from the dropdown to pin it.
- Enter a description
- Click on Pin it.
- How to Find Images to Pin?

You have the option to pin images from a wide range of sources.

Keep on searching and repining the latest popular images (You must keep on connecting with maximum people. It is really good to use popular appealing images that can lure other people to repin the images on their boards and like them).

Search images that other community members have repined several times and repin these pins regularly to your boards.

Find images that are unique, funny, surprising and appealing. These type of pins have the tendency to go viral (Each time somebody repins a photo, the particular board it belongs to is visible to the re-pinner with the option to follow the board or the profile. This is very fascinating for a business owner as it gives a chance to open up the business profile to maximum people and higher re-pins means that more people will view and visit the profile and business website)

For keeping the users engaged and refreshing the content, always pin images from the latest trending themes and topics.

Stay in touch with the social media websites in order to view the interests of people.

For generating the maximum interest of the users, pin range of your business products and services with relevant info graphics, guides and how to do information.

Find images on Pinterest that relate to the board theme you desire to add a pin to. (Enter the keywords in the 'search' box right at the top of Pinterest page. This will be a really helpful starting point for you to begin exploring)

Pin few examples about the top 10 features as several online magazines as well as newspapers have very unique ' The top 10... ' features that include things like top 10 hairstyles, top 5 resorts, top 7 astonishing facts etc.

- Boost Traffic on Pinterest
- Add relevant Keywords to your:
- User name
- 'About' section of profile
- Board Names
- Description of boards

- File Names of images
- Description of images

Always add links to the information and captions of your posts. These links have great worth, as they remain live. It does not matter how many times the images are repined; they will generate traffic for your business website.

Include a link in the pin by editing the uploaded images. Use different techniques including contests to increase the engagement, like Pin to Win.

Add links of your other social media accounts on Pinterest.

Use the 'Follow me on Pinterest' button for your Twitter and Facebook accounts (It makes it quite easy to share pines on different social media websites)

Add the tab of Pinterest on your Facebook page (You can do this by using Facebook developer application or you can visit the http://www.woobox.com

to get a free application.

Do not forget to add a 'Pin It' button on your website and blog.

Send invitations to friends via email, Twitter, Facebook or search them on Pinterest.

Follow the users and Pinterest boards that have large number of follower base.

Follow back the ones who have re-pinned any of your pins or who have followed you.

Do not just focus on pin or repin. Be a humble user and healthy contributor to the social community of Pinterest by liking, commenting, sharing and thanking the users who add pins from your boards.

Share interesting and unique images on Face book and Twitter.

Monitor your Pinterest statistics

By using the Pinterest and Google Analytics, scrutinize your performance on Pinterest.

Get to know about very useful aspects like:

- Which days and time period that you pin on, fetch the best output?
- Which boards are famous and have more followers? Then you can use these boards frequently.

Capitalize On Visual Interest

Placement of boards has great significance. Place the popular, significant and inter related boards in the centre of your page including the top and the middle. (A study by Mashable helped to give a priceless insight in to how people view the boards of individual users on Pinterest. Most people focus on the centre of the screen and they move eyes straight on the middle of the boards to get number of views)

Choose engaging and attractive images for each board cover.

Make sure that all the prominent boards are lying above the fold (the top of any page when visible on the screen)

Refresh your boards by changing the board covers and arrange them at regular intervals.

Ensure that you position seasonal boards in the top row if you have any.

By making a proper Pinterest Business account, you can greatly increase the number of sale opportunities as well as reinforce the relationship with the potential customers. The visual features of Pinterest have proven record of accomplishment of engaging a viewer to become a customer. By staying involved on Pinterest, your business can get a huge number of benefits by more traffic and better sales growth.

Conclusion

Pinterest is an interactive socializing website that allows you to keep track of things online by "pinning" images on your board, just like you pin things on a notice board. With almost 100 million users, it is the fastest growing social media website today. It saves all of your "pins" on your page, allows you to share your pins with friends, re-pin your friends' pins, and see strangers' public pins that are of interest to you. You can describe Pinterest as a socializing platform based on images and videos of your interest.

People use Pinterest for a number of reasons like sports, fashion, cooking, photography, art, and for other interests. It is also a great platform to share your passions and obsessions about your favorite books, movies, and TV series.